Times Knew Roamin'

Poems by Marybeth Niederkorn

Kansas City   Spartan Press   Missouri

Spartan Press
Kansas City, Missouri
spartanpresskc.com

Copyright (c) Marybeth Niederkorn, 2018
First Edition 1 3 5 7 9 10 8 6 4 2
ISBN: 978-1946642-91-2
LCCN: 2018967937

Design, edits and layout: Jason Ryberg
Cover image and author photo: Kassi Jackson
All rights reserved. No part of this publication may be reproduced or transmitted in any form or by any means, electronic or mechanical, including photocopying, recording or by info retrieval system, without prior written permission from the author.

First and foremost, I want to thank my husband, Dave, who, when we were first dating and he was introducing me to people, opened with "This is Marybeth, my girlfriend, she's a writer and is going to be even more successful than she already is." He's pretty much the best. Unflinching support.

My writing partners, Shana Scott and Joshua de Vries, read every poem in here and, even though both of them would rather I was handing fiction to them, they gave excellent feedback.

Initially I was planning this collection as a chapbook, and had fewer than 20 poems in it. Then Jason Ryberg asked me if I had a full-length manuscript so it could go on the publication schedule for 2019, and I said, "...Sure." A few months later, I had 50. His support and interest are literally the reasons this book exists.

The extremely talented Kassi Jackson lent her photographic skills to this project, too. Her photo graces the cover, and she managed to get an author photo of me that I really love—a major achievement.

My parents are awesome. I could go on for years about their encouragement. And I will.

Of course, there's Richie Narvaez. He ran an online poetry journal, The Journal of Asinine Poetry, that, in 2001, was the first real outlet beyond my tiny pond of recognition to give my work a platform. And Richie kept me going when I wanted to give up, by keeping writing fun for me, and including a poem of mine in an anthology and inviting me to read at the Bowery Poetry Club in Manhattan. It was an incredible honor and I'm proud to know him.

I would not like to thank my black cat, who is asleep on my left forearm and getting annoyed with me for typing around him.

Finally, I want to extend a most heartfelt thanks to my mentor and friend, Susan Swartwout, who saved my life when she asked if I wanted to go to graduate school.

-MN

"Highway 32 West" and "The Moon Rocks Over" appeared in Volume 2 of T*he Gasconade Review: Missouri is a Ghost-Shaped Thing.*

"To the Man in the Blue Neon with Wide White Stripes" appeared in Volume 7 of *Trailer Park Quarterly.*

CONTENTS

Exit 102 to Old Appleton at 117 / 1

I Was Going to Call This "The Woods" but the Point Is in the Bag / 5

Highway Thoughts / 6

Vulture / 8

Highway 32 West / 10

New with You / 12

Stranded / 14

As I Read Student Papers / 15

How to Write a Slam Poem / 16

Even the City Has Its Limits / 17

Distance Flattens / 19

Modesty / 21

On a Dumpster / 22

The Worst Literary Journal / 24

Easy for Me to Say / 26

She Is So Many Women / 28

Square Root of For Is Too / 30

Wanty / 32

Res Extensa / 34

Therapy / 38

Different Infinities / 40

Long Stretch / 42

Learning Isn't Teaching / 44

Where Do Commas Go? / 45

Fight the Monster Without Becoming It / 48

OK, Fine, This Is Where Commas Go / 49

I Finally Understand / 52

Fault Line / 53

Roundabout / 55

Junction City / 59

To the Man in the Blue Neon with
  Wide White Stripes / 60

Sliding Doors / 62

No Line / 64

Don't Half Ass Your Cheatery / 66

Stomping Grounds / 68

Every Fry a Bag Fry / 70

The Moon Rocks Over / 71

Times Knew Roamin'

To Dave, who doesn't appear in this much,
but who is the reason this was possible.

Exit 102 to Old Appleton at 117

I.
I refuse to listen to audiobooks, even
though I could easily get a free trial
for a digital audiobook service, or
maybe borrow an audiobook from
the public library back home. I did
try that, once. I haven't read enough
Jane Austen to feel legitimate in my
English-major pomposity—I can't
call it street cred, because, come
on. I have two degrees. I drive a Civic.
An old Civic. I might refer to it as Civic
Doody if I lacked a little more self-respect,
or voted more frequently. But Jane Austen,
I borrowed Pride and Prejudice on twelve
discs, but the first disc got stuck in the player,
and I'm not sure how to get it out, so I'm just
racking up overdue fines at a nickel a day until
magically the damn thing leaps out of my CD
player, or a solution occurs to me, one better than
duct tape sticky side out on a ruler, which, I am
aware, is probably not the best idea.

So, sure, that didn't work out so well, but what about
a digital download, on my tablet, plugged in to the audio
jack, using the retractable cable I bought for that
exact purpose? I'm sure that'd be fine

until I zone out around Oak Ridge and fall
asleep before I hit the exit for the Cowboy Church,
which I thought was a hallucination the first
few times I saw it, but since then I've seen several
bumper stickers for it around town, mostly on
black pickup trucks and heavy-duty SUVs
that have dirt on the rear bumper, as though
this sport utility vehicle probably actually
sees some real sport or perhaps even utility,
so I'm fairly convinced it's a real thing.

II.
For that matter, I also refuse to drive over the
speed limit. I'm never on the interstate with
a lot of traffic. No one's heading north at 8:30
a.m. except semi trucks and government vehicles.
I'm guessing social workers. There are several
facilities between Cape and Perryville that workers
have to travel between, if I understand my friends
in the field correctly, and, yes, there is every
possibility that I do not.

Could be these are operatives, the kind who
don't have names so much as they have
designations. I don't mean to sound paranoid,
but I do wonder about how agents live their lives.
I wonder about how everyone else lives their lives.
Each and every driver and passenger around me
is heading to an important place that I will
never know. I haven't paid enough attention to the

drivers themselves, not of the big rigs anyway. I can't
tell if they recognize me from trip to trip, or if they're
even the same people. I suppose that's snobby of me.
Or is it just self-centered? I am absorbed while on
this stretch. I'm thinking about the landscape, thinking
about the highway funding that allowed this four-laner
to be brought into existence, with dynamite blasting
through bedrock, with asphalt being churned out at an
alarming rate, with Highway 61 being replaced by this
interstate, this shrine to efficiency, this artery of the
American dream. But arteries take blood away
from the heart, so what's that say about me?

III.
I won't talk on my cell either. For one thing,
no one's available right now. They're either
working their straight jobs, their nine-to-fives,
their steady paycheck providers, or they're
raising children so working to get them into
the day's routine, or they're doing literally
anything but talking to me on the phone.
Probably having adventures. Sigh. Also,
8:30 a.m. is a weird time to be on the phone.
It just is.

IV.
I try, I really do, not to fixate on the roadkill.
Counting the armadillos crushed or exploded
by passing traffic whose drivers probably didn't
even realize they'd ended a tiny life, or care if

they did realize, feels pretty macabre, and I try
to convince myself that I'm not mesmerized
by the darker side of life.
There are fifteen. Oh,
and a hawk.
The carcasses just roll on by
or maybe it's me that's passing.

I Was Going to Call This "The Woods" but the Point Is in the Bag

I'm heading into the woods, but
instead of being swathed in a red
cape, with my picnic basket, my
dessert for Grandmother, I'm in
my green Civic, with an insulated
bag, blue, with the words *English
is COOL!* in white lettering, above
a textbook company logo. It was
free when I was in graduate school,
and like so many gifts I've been
given, I took it, seeing a reflection
of myself in its cerulean handles,
its fabric. It even has pockets. And
beyond that, it works great as a
carry-sack for four bottles of wine,
and a little bit of cheese. Unfortunately
that's not what's inside today. It's just
my lunch, and a soda, and an ice pack
to keep everything chill on my hour-plus
drive. But at least it has my name
in all caps, in black permanent marker,
with an exclamation point. That way we
know whose it is.

Highway Thoughts
for Dave, my awesome husband

I fell in love with you
in the spaces between.
I think about that a lot,
on the road, where I see
your face in every green
leaf, your heart in every
tree trunk, your eyes
in every space of sky
between the clouds.

I fell in love with you
where life happens.

I fell in love with you
where the lonely places
weren't lonely anymore.

We say fell in love. Like
a tree, a harvested animal,
a successful hunt. Mown
down. But you and I, we
weren't like that. We grew,
from within, an acorn
splitting a boulder
as it rooted and spread.

That's not exactly what I mean.

But love is the building of
a language, and the expression,
a language that hums instead
of speaks. No wonder I resisted.
Words have always meant more
than music, to me.
                        And yet I dance.

You remind me why.

Vulture

It's hard to like a scavenger.
His finery isn't streamlined, his
feet are stained in shades of offal.
It's altogether off-putting, where a
predator stares keenly into you, sees
prey worth attaining, worth pursuing.
Scavengers are ungainly, ragged things,
flopping about, searching, seeking, never
quite getting the laser-beam stare perfected.
But when morning sun catches them
soaring, lights their broken edges
afire, for a moment, just one
fleeting moment, stench
of death evaporates,
the hate the world
bears for them
slips away,
and what's
left could
almost,
almost
be exactly
what's
needed.
Also, vultures

use projectile
vomiting to
get others
to leave
them
alone,
and I
can get
behind
that.

Highway 32 West

They say a journey of a thousand steps begins with a single mile, or maybe I have that wrong, but it feels right, on this stretch of 32 that has no shoulder but plenty of logging trucks. I can picture myself catapulting end over end into the sedge and pine forests on either side of the highway, one side bisected by railroad tracks, the other with its furrowed valley that I get a vague sense of disapproval from. I'm not sure if I'm projecting. I'm not sure of much, here, with my travel mug of lukewarm coffee and my radio turned all the way down because the static is almost worse than the country music or the station out of St. Louis that *You never know what you'll hear next!* which *frankly* sounds more than a little ominous.

Or maybe I'm picking up on the rage coming at me from the redneck in his dooley pickup truck. Spellcheck tells me dooley isn't a word, and Google is pretty sure I mean *dually*, but search results seem to be telling me that a *dually* pickup truck is not what I assumed a dooley was, i.e., a pickup truck with dual wheels in back, often accompanied by chrome truck nuts. *Truck nuts,* I might add, are a thing I assumed *had* to be fictional, since I first saw them on a cartoon show about redneck debauchery, which has some elements of satire, but no, no, *truck nuts are real.* People really do set out with the sole purpose of purchasing or procuring a dangly set of faux testicles to hang from their truck's trailer hitch, and then they just kind of drive around with them on, presumably yelling *WOOEEE!* more frequently than your average driver, because he's behind the wheel of a dooley pickup truck, freshly gross from muddin'. It's a lifestyle choice, I guess— a lifestyle choice that also involves shouting obscenities at a blonde in a Civic who drives the speed limit, *sensibly*. Like, aggressively sensibly. Not that I mind being screamed at by a man whose bumper stickers carry vile messages, who probably wouldn't scream at me in any other context, unless I was walking alone on a street. Then probably he'd take it upon himself to remind me that damn, my hot ass is hot, and he thanks me for leaving the kitchen so he could see it. From across the street. Where I can't punch him. Because *courage* is totally in this guy's wheelhouse. Yeah, scream at the driver ahead of you with the staff parking permit for a community college. Yeah, scream at the driver whose car is clearly just this side of falling completely apart, as evidenced by the missing bumper cover and the giant dent from where some damn kid was out skateboarding (probably) and fell on the hood, which crumpled like a paper sack, but more expensively. Yeah, scream at the driver who isn't moving slowly solely to piss you off, but who is acutely aware of those logging trucks, and of the farm-implements sales yards (plural) between here and the next major highway. It's not that I want to rear-end a combine, or a tractor with a back-end loader whose metal spikes are bigger around than my leg, and would be aimed directly into the driver's seat, where, you might have noticed, *I happen to be sitting.* I guess I think about things that other people maybe don't consider while they're trying to run over the chick in the Honda?

New with You

I'm not complaining, really I'm not. But
I am sincerely looking forward to the day
when someone I haven't seen for a couple
years casually asks *So what's new with
you?*

meaning, *What haven't you been telling Facebook about?*

and my response
is an honest *Nothing really, and you?*

Because as of right now, I'm lying through
my teeth when I tell people that there's nothing
worth reporting, that I've been telling the world
everything worth knowing about me and what
I'm up to.

Yes, I did love grad school. Rebuilt my life
in and with a firestorm.

Priceless. I wouldn't have done it any other way.

But even though I'm proud of what I've accomplished,
even though I'm thrilled that I can hold my head
above water (sure, my feet are kicking furiously,
I'm Esther Williamsing the shit out of this, but that
is so beside the point), I gotta tell you, I'm

also really looking forward to the day when my achievements are all old news. Uh.

                                          Wait a minute.

Maybe I've been thinking about this a little bit wrongheadedly. Maybe instead of hoping that everything settles down for me just a little bit, maybe I ought to be thinking that I'm finally right about ready to get started.

Stranded

I don't know why there's a beauty standard what
says long blonde hair is desirable on a woman,
because for me, it's a never-ending parade
through golden spiderwebs, a continual
state of disheveled dress, as I pull fine strands
of burnt-gold filament from my clothing, chairs,
pillows, really anything I graze by
with even an iota of static electric charge.

I realize it's probably not science to think
my hair is attracted to fabric because fabric
holds a charge, slim along the surface, a
charge that doesn't gather and spark unless
someone who's averse to haircuts
wanders past, shedding and unaware

As I Read Student Papers

I long for the days of yesterday's society, when
we had fewer things all around us, at home, at
work, even at school. Learning was easier, then,
when pitfalls did not befall us, when grammar
and spelling were left unchecked, when sentences
fragmented only along fissures opened with regard
to, in essence, something very necessary
which no one ever thought about, ever. No one.
Ever!

Those were the days when everyone knew
to set the margins to one inch all around, when
the times were New and Roman, the spacing
double. The header was the best! Last name,
page number, right aligned, *correctly*. It goes
without saying that saying things begets sayings,
which might have led to a thesis statement, but
to write a thesis statement, I'd need both a thesis
and a statement, so.

In conclusion, my conclusion is a concluding
conclusion, and I long for the days of yesterday's
society, when my thesis statement was copied
and pasted directly from the beginning, and none
of the body came from Wikipedia. I swear.

How to Write a Slam Poem

Get some anger.
Sit on it.
Let it fester, gangrenous and true,
in your soul like a snake bite abscessed.
Then, when you're pretty sure
you can almost, almost let it laugh
at itself, lance that boil, let it pour
forth with pus and water, streaming from
your side, not quite in a stream of consciousness
but in more of a stream of dark, dark humor,
a humor like bile, darkish green and vomited
on the floor next to the toilet
of poetic expression.

Even the City Has Its Limits

I keep thinking I'll see changes closer to
the edge, the way I see changes in myself
when I'm close to my own limits, but mine
are not defined by population or property
lines, taxation, voter rolls or anything like that.

Houses sit farther apart, out here, ditches'
weeds are taller, and the road signs are more
likely to be in code, letter and number names,
than named for someone, something.

Once I saw a stray chicken out here, its feathers
green and russet. Reminded me of an oil slick on
a mud puddle. Mud's red here, you know. Some
say it's the iron content in the soil, but since this
up here is in the lead belt, I'd say it's the blood of
broken dreams.

My limits are more about snapping, about the
length between my angry breaths, the distance
from one to ten as I count it out to keep from
screaming, or to keep my blood pressure spikes
in check against the migraine blossom igniting
like so much lighter fluid poured against my skull.

Of course, if the city had migraines, they would probably not manifest quite the same way. Lights flashing in the periphery, crippling pain pressing all activity down, down, until it's not possible anymore—that feels more like an upward limit than an outward one.

Distance Flattens

The thing with being far away, in any one direction, is
it flattens in the rearview, or the fore. I can see clouds
when I'm flying through them, or I can see shapes from
the ground. But it's the same, from up there, seeing down.

I think the same is true of the future versus the past,
the page versus the actions, the relationship versus the
memory. And I am totally fine with that. I've never been
one to live entirely on the page or entirely in the action.
I stand to one side, watching as things happen rather
than stepping in, as much as to understand more of the
human experience as to distance myself from it.

It's part of why I'm enjoying the drive, is seeing in the
rearview, backwards and distorted but still a reflection.
That, and the view ahead, stretching for asphalt miles,
trees and heavy weeds along the shoulder. I shrug off
comparisons to other poets who've made long drives,
poets who found themselves as much as they found
the highway's freedom. There isn't a lot of freedom
to be had for the asking, here. This is soybean country,
where beans are grown and tofu mostly sneered at (I
speak for people who aren't vegans, obviously; myself
I'm not opposed to tofu but you won't see me ordering it
on a pizza).

It's easy to wonder, here, on the country's outskirts, whether liberal views are held in urban areas because people have to live with everyone, directly in their faces, so the homeless problem is less an academic one and more a *there's a woman lives in the alley next to my workplace who urinates on the building if she gets annoyed at me, which she does, regularly* reality. It's easy to be outside a city and think solutions to society's ills are an imperative rather than less important than the barley crop.

Modesty

I think it's weird how Bugs Bunny
walks around naked all the time, but
as soon as he's in drag, he's suddenly
Captain Modesty when a clothing piece
falls off. I like to think this is a scathing
critique of the different expectations of
men and women, in our society, but I'm
not altogether sure that's what's going on
there. I think maybe he's just getting
really into his role—that modesty
exists within women's clothing,
I guess. It's hard to know with
cartoon rabbits.

On a Dumpster

SPA BOX the Dumpster says, sprayed white across its blistered green surface, J/K it says as an afterthought. It's on a flatbed and we're playing tag on I-55 north, the semi pulling a trailer with two industrial-green receptacles that have lived a cycle in a parking lot somewhere, ostensibly, and I am staring at those three groups of letters, transfixed, as the semi speeds and slows beside me, jogs into the lane ahead of me, jigs back, drops behind, pulls alongside me again. After twenty miles of this, I'm thinking, who in the world grabbed a can of white spray paint, looked at a Dumpster in a parking lot, adrift in a sea of concrete, litter, the sick greens of weeds and antifreeze stains, had a thought to immortalize some great words, but what? What words could sum up the pinnacle of this person's thoughts, this person who clearly had a desire to etch an echo of their thoughts onto the face of time itself, of human history? Who was this faceless someone whose finger pressed a trigger and white paint splatted onto the surface of this shrine to human over-consumption?

Also, this shrine is gross.

But what prompted this? It's summer, now, so probably this person walked past the Dumpster at least once, and noticed how stinky, how intense the stench that wafted from the great shadowy depths of this hulking ugly thing, and a thought began to form, a little joke, maybe even repeated to coworkers who'd also taken out the trash and smelled the smells themselves, and it became a long-running thing, a joke to end all jokes, a crowning glory of a funny thing, and maybe one night, maybe those same coworkers got together in the parking lot and shared a bottle of some cheap but efficient hooch (I'm hoping it wasn't Mad Dog) until one of them got the bright and bold idea to get into their truck and grab out the can of white spray paint, and spray SPA BOX on the SPA BOX they'd been kidding each other about for days, maybe weeks, but one coworker, we'll call her Tiffani (because she seems like the kind of person who would be nicknamed Tiffy but would claim to hate it), Tiffani insisted J/K was necessary because otherwise someone might think, I mean it's pretty unlikely but what if someone thought SPA BOX was not a joke, climbed in, thinking they were going to get some fancy spa treatment, you know how people are, they're just so dumb about things sometimes, so if we don't J/K it, *there could be a tragedy, you guys.*

I for one am glad Tiffy insisted, because it's really entertaining me today.

Thank you, Tiffy, wherever you are.

The Worst Literary Journal

I have a secret.
Sometimes, when I'm doing my job,
responding to papers students have
turned in to our online commenting
system, and I've read the same clichés
fourteen papers in a row, I lapse into
pretending I am the editor
of the world's worst literary
journal, titled *In Today's Society,*
where students' work is celebrated,
no apostrophe is used correctly,
commas are just … everywhere,
three-syllable words are all exactly
wrong, logical structures are, well,
not structures at all,
and MLA format is right out.
Spacing wouldn't be double.
Book titles would be, I dunno,
what's a quotation mark, again?
Isn't that what comes on the
end of a question, direct or not?
What does italicized mean?

The margins would not be 1" on
all sides.

Nor would the font be
12-point TNR.

TNR!

I explain what that stands for
at least once per week, in life,

in this world in which we live

in, at this current time and place.

…

See,
I'm already
ready
to

                                        contribute.

Easy for Me to Say

When no one has ever told you that you are smart enough to do the thing, when in fact you have heard from early on that you are *not* smart enough to do the thing, I can see how you'd think perhaps you aren't smart enough to do the thing, even though, my student, you *are* smart enough to do the thing.

But it's easy for you, they tell me, and they are right, it is easy for me, but that does not make it impossible for them. Until I try to explain.

In a punctuation quiz, multiple choice, I'm called to a station where a student struggles. I ask *"What is your question?"* and on the screen, the quiz is asking the student to identify the semicolon. *"Well,"* I say, *"is it A, B, C, or D?" "No,"* the reply, *"what is that word?" "Semi... colon?" Right. Well,* I say, utterly at a loss, having pronounced it, and not sure where to go from here, *"did you read the chapter?" "It didn't have this word,"* the reply. *"I cannot give you a quiz answer,"* I say, and I can't, so I go back to my desk. I open to the chapter. There's a semicolon, all right, but not with a definition.

My boss would know what to do, how to address this, so I just send an email noting the student's name and question, and can the boss do anything to help. He'll see it later.

And that's kind of an outlier. The questions you, the student, ask are typically more mundane, more nuts and bolts, the kind of thing someone with a master's degree in English *should* be able to tell you. What's a predicate? What's an intransitive verb? Where do commas go? *What is a dependent clause?*

So many times I am tempted to answer *"The English language is not a language at all, but a complex system trying to trick you into following rules that aren't rules, because our grammar rules are more conventions than anything."*

I don't think that would help you, though.

She Is So Many Women

She enters the lab, shoulders dropped,
messy ponytail, books and notes clutched
in defense against a world she has learned
to distrust. *I have an appointment with
you, I think,* she tells me, I nod, we sit.
She isn't crying, yet. That's later. For now,
we're talking about her term paper, only her
term paper, and why she chose the topic
of domestic abuse. I nod. She's about my
age, maybe a little older, or younger. She's
been Mom longer than she can remember. I
tell her she's got me there, but she should go on.

Her husband doesn't like that she's here,
she says. Her hands are folded, twisting
in an invisible wind, but I hear it. I felt it,
feel it, radiating from her. He's just
demanding, she says. He's just
frustrated in his life right now, he's just
seven different ways to say abusive.

She's apologetic. She shouldn't be burdening
me with this. I shake my head, remind her
that most of what my job is, is steadying
students on their educational journey. And
sometimes education isn't about what's in
your lesson plans and homework.

Growing beyond yourself is education, too.
Growing beyond your fear, growing beyond
your reluctance to give up on what you've
poured your life into, growing beyond your
inability to accept that this has gone beyond
not working and is heading solidly toward
probably going to kill me territory.

She thinks she's not as ready as she is.

She thinks this paper is going to be harder than
it is. She wants me to tell her that she needs to
scrap this draft, that being married is what she needs
to do, that the disintegration is all her fault, that
she just needs to suck it up and live like an adult,
that happiness is a fairy tale and she should have
outgrown that by now.

But I will not. I cannot. I will not be responsible
for dashing the tiny ember of hope she has stoked
within herself. He's been doing his best to do that
to her, and I
will not. She
will finish
this draft.
And turn
it
in.

Square Root of For Is Too

I'm not going to say that my math anxiety is
rooted in anything other than years and years
and years
of failing miserably at every attempt
I have ever made to think sequentially
when faced with an algebraic expression.
Hmph.

An *expression* in English terminology is nothing more
than a quick saying, a shorthand for a cultural touchstone,
a reference, if you will. English, I understand. English, I
comprehend. With English, I will use every method I can
think of to express what I want to express.

Meaning, in words, is not quantifiable, not the way meaning
in mathematics is quantifiable, and I have long been jealous
of that. If I had the ability to create a calculus that would
quantify meaning in words and expressions, maybe that
would end a lifelong struggle. I'm not arrogant enough
to think I'm the only one with this problem.

But no. I do not have the chops to create a new calculus
entirely from scratch, the way philosopher Jeremy
Bentham did with the hedonistic calculus, when he
was creating utilitarianism. That concept enthralled me.
It showed that I could make judgments on what to do
using exactly the information I had at hand. Unbelievable.

Which might be why it's not exactly common knowledge. Interesting thought exercise. Less useful than its name suggests.

I who had wondered for ages how to express my frustration, unable to explain where meaning came from in language, since, after all, words are only rearrangements of the same set of 26 letters, and applying syntax to that arrangement creates a system, sure, but it's all nebulous and fraught with misunderstanding and inability to accurately convey exactly what the intended meaning was. Not like math.

So sure, I'm a touch jealous of mathematicians and their ability to quantifiably express what amounts to a concrete concept, where the best and closest I can do is a poem about the poem-writing process.

Wanty

I need to do good in this class, she says, bouncing from foot to foot, impatient, not meeting my eyes. *Well,* I say, and she doesn't hear me. She's already asking me another question, about how to make her paragraph say what she wants it to say.

She's been assigned a paragraph, that's all, a single paragraph with five sentences, describing a loved pet. Hers starts out with five words about her dog. The cursor blinks, waiting, and she's caving under the pressure.

She wants me to help. Help, help, all I do is help, but I'm not sure my help is actually helping. Not this student, anyway.

She comes in on my shift, every time, and stands at my desk for most of her session. *Why?* I ask, and she cannot or will not answer. She doesn't hear me. Am I not loud enough, or is what's roaring through her head drowning me out? I can tell she doesn't think she belongs here, that she thinks college is for smart people, and that she has wasted her chances in life by getting addicted to drugs, but she is doing better, bound and determined. She's in treatment. She's in school. She's in drug court. She's using chances. But as much as I admire that, I cannot

write her story for her. I am no ghostwriter. I am
a tutor. I am a teacher's helper. I am a support
person for the software's teaching. I am here
to tell a student to read the chapter again. I
am here to tell the student the same information
with different words. I am here to try to flip the
switch powering the lightbulb now dim, soon
bright, or at least that's the hope.

And today, I am growing tired of her antics,
her pacing the room instead of working, her
asking me for countless endless help, and when
she steps up to my desk for the eleventh time in
fifteen minutes, I answer her, she goes away, and
my coworker at the next desk hands me a piece
of paper, face down, and walks away.

I am not needy, I am wanty, says a white cat's
caption, reaching for a plate of what I can
only assume is food. And I laugh. I laugh
so hard tears are forming and I can't help
but lean into it, sagging face-first into my
keyboard, where I have been typing in
between her visits, correcting and suggesting
edits for student work, and when I lift my head,
there's a note that reads *ghghghghgjk—Marybeth,
3:06 p.m.*

Res Extensa

Rene Descartes was a French philosopher in the 1600s, a devout Roman Catholic, a mathematician, a soldier. He never married but carried a snotty smirk under his pencil mustache. His heavy nose and supercilious stare inspired me not to envy or imitation, but to spine-deep shudders when his name came up. My aversion to ol' Renny, as I liked to call him, was probably because of my inherent dislike of everything I am told I should like. I was studying toward a philosophy degree at the turn of the millennium, under professors all white, all but one male, all middle- to upper-class.

Yes, he's the father of modern philosophy, but why does everything have to spring from a father? Where is the mother in this scenario?

What I loved about my philosophy classes is, the professors worked hard to place the texts in context, with history, biography, sequence. We focused mainly on Western philosophy, and that was fine by me.

As one of the only women majoring in a small department, and one of the only people majoring only in philosophy at a university without a pre-law program, I had no real interest in political science or an art degree as my side piece, as most everyone else was doing. I started with a minor in computer science and went through more than a few others before landing on creative writing and a whole lot of electives to reach my hours requirement for graduation.

I didn't have a lot to prove, either, which was different than a lot of what I observed in my fellow students. I sat through endless debates in classes where my fellows had not read the material, clearly, but still wanted the payoff of being *right*. I was less interested in being right than I was in playing on the intellectual swingset built by dead Europeans hundreds of years before I was born.

I assumed for years that philosophy was as easy for them as it was for me. I assumed that the other students could just as easily understand what was in the treatises on man and the human condition.

When I wrote the first few pages of *Meditations! The Rene Descartes Musical Comedy*, I had a moment of clarity, understanding that maybe *serious philosopher* wasn't quite in my job description. Oh, but *humorous philosopher*, that, I could get behind.

And one concept of Descartes' that did stick with me was that of res extensa, res cogitans.

A big chunk of Descartes' philosophy dealt with mind-body dualism, OK, a distinction between the substance of body and the substance of mind. For Descartes, the mind acted upon the body and was not a part of it, even though the mind suffused the body (muscle memory, you see, is mind operating in the body).

I found that interesting but limited.

Descartes also had this thing about attributes. An object has attributes, or features, or observable characteristics, or traits. Descartes talked about a ball of wax, and its fragrance, its shape, its weight, its solidity, and how when heat was applied to the wax and the ball's attributes all fell away, he could still observe the wax to be wax, but not the ball anymore.

Although the wax could be reformed once it cooled.

Attributes and objects were to each other as mind and body were to each other, I thought, where the two were distinct but acted on each other.

Neat.

Res extensa was Descartes' term for the extension of self into the body. Res cogitans was the term for extension of the mind into the universe.

I know that's not how it's translated. I know *res cogitans* is *thinking substance* and *res extensa* is *extended substance* but those definitions feel dusty and exclusionary, and philosophy, for me, is vibrant, alive.

I like the idea of mind extending into the universe, OK.

So here's Descartes, living in 16th century Deventer, in the Netherlands (he moved around a lot), writing about two substances, one thinking, one extending, entwined parallels working for a goal of *living*.

My thinking on this, in 21st century Cape Girardeau, in the United States (I haven't moved around a lot), is that the problem with Descartes' res extensa is, he didn't have a car to drive.

I think about this a lot as I'm driving, my skinny shell of metal and glass and upholstered padding and plastic skimming over endless miles of pavement. *I'm like a very speedy hermit crab,* I think, only my car is either clean inside and out or messy, depending on my mental state, and I can feel it almost as a physical pain when something is wrong with the car's body or internals. I worry over it, clucking at its worn tires or stained floor mats, feeling its energy drop low when fuel reserves need refilling. When it breaks down, I break down. The feelings flow from outside in.

Therapy

It's raining today, makes the drive stretch like warm taffy, sends my mind in loping cycles, working that taffy like it's going to be so many vanilla chunks wrapped in wax paper, delicious at the fair but a few weeks later they're fragrant rocks I could break a tooth on, chewing.

It reminds me of my brief flirtation with therapy, when my now-ex husband told me our marriage needed work, said he was willing to go to a therapy session with me, but only if I would promise to make a real effort, did I understand, the kind of effort that would save this relationship, and I was like *Sure* so we went, and he spent an hour trying to humiliate me, telling the therapist things he knew I didn't want to talk about, like he thought that maybe he could intimidate me into staying with him because he had *dirt* on me, did I understand, dirt on me, and at the end, when we were done, when she said, *There, do you feel like giving her a hug?* and he said *No, I don't want to touch her,* we walked outside and I said *What was that* and he told me he didn't think therapy was such a great idea since it would be too expensive, and I pointed out to him that this was his idea, and how could he put a price on our marriage like that, and he said if I didn't spend so much of his money, we'd be better off, and I pointed out that I had quit my job at his request so I could as he said *take care of* him, and I am probably remembering this conveniently, but something tells me probably not, too.

And even though these memories are painful,
obnoxious, that I would let myself be treated that way,
that I would even encourage it in a bid to punish myself
for things I was convinced I'd done to deserve it,
to preserve a situation I chose and in my pride would not
relinquish, they still smell faintly of vanilla, but instead
of trying to eat them, maybe I'll line my driveway with
them instead.

The crunch is satisfying.

Different Infinities

I was a smart kid, intellectually curious, I've
learned the term is, and learning not only came
easily to me, but was as natural and necessary
as breathing. I took it in, I exhaled. I spent
hours, days, years in the library, its dusty
midcentury-modern leftovers as much a
part of what was happening between me
and countless hardback books with grainy
gray and black images and important
serif font as the widening of my intellectual
horizons. I was in a gifted program where I
did special projects and science experiments
and read books and wrote out problems in my
chicken-scratch longhand. Dad and I spent
countless hours with weather-predicting kits
and a microscope and a telescope and our
family computer and family encyclopedia
and he never told me a question I asked was
anything other than interesting, if not answerable.

I hoped adulthood would be more of the same.

For awhile, it was. I studied philosophy, working
with professors who saw beyond the pedestrian, the
mundane, with other gifted-class refugees who, like
me, remembered fourth-grade afternoons where the
other students were struggling to learn long division

or state capitols and we were the ones thinking about how much fun it would be to learn calculus someday. Then I landed in a writing lab, teaching 18-year-olds how to form sentences, how to punctuate, how to separate main ideas from supporting evidence.

As an early undergraduate, I took a course on modern essay writing, and from the beginning of that semester to the end, I evolved. I morphed from a place of not understanding how to write a personal essay to writing one that won an award. *You ought to be a TA*, my professor said, and I of course laughed at that, because I am not a teacher, I told him, so why would I teach a college course? But he insisted, *The best way to learn something is to teach it to someone else, and you can reach real heights with writing. Learn all you can.*

Now, I'm sitting at my desk, words across my screen, giving structural feedback to a student who barely understands how words work, trying to fit everything I know about writing and words into a single sentence that is both supportive and encouraging, and I remember two salient points.

One, education never stops.
Two, not all education is gathering facts.

Long Stretch

Before Meadow Heights, before the turn
to Sedgewickville, or Daisy, there's a long
stretch of empty highway punctuated by
farmland and houses, not so frequent
as you might think. It's here that my mind
travels without my permission, and it's here
that I find myself screaming at you. Not
because you hurt me or whatever, not because
our relationship was supposed to be a forever
kind of thing, not even because you were
not great to me almost from the start. That
doesn't bother me so much.

Four years out
from the moment I stopped drowning, from
the moment I lifted my head and pushed
my feet under me to find the water I had thought
was endless depth was shallower than I was.
I'm not shallow, by the way.

That's what I'm
shouting about. I'm shouting that you did your
level best to convince me that I am many
people I am not. I am not undeserving of love.
I am not unworthy of respect. I am not cold,
or manly, or any of the other traits you assigned
to me to keep me firmly in check, under

your will. I am not a failure at writing, a
failure at holding a job, a failure at achieving
that which I hold dearest. After years of thinking
about this, reflecting on it, ruminating, I've
concluded that failure isn't failure when
what you're pouring your efforts into
isn't worth winning.

I'm sure
every person who's ever written a breakup poem
ever has felt the same attraction to simplifying
a lifetime's worth of interactions into nothing
more than labels repeated often enough that
they lose all meaning. Like *time machine.* Say
time machine to yourself fifteen times.
Now keep saying it.
Say it again and again until, like *emotional
abuse,* like *jerkface,* like *destroyed my old
life so I had to build a new one which was
surprisingly liberating considering how hard
it was to build but maybe that had more to do
with the slobby contrary-minded monkey on
my back the first time through—*
yeah, *time machine* loses all meaning too.

Learning Isn't Teaching

The textbook creaks open to chapter
2, titled *How to Write the 5-Paragraph
Essay,* subtitled with bullets, every one
even more of a snore, and I remember
this moment so clearly because I was
the only one in my fifth-grade class
eagerly devouring the suggestions
for success at the chapter's end. Maybe
I should have been more critical and
less wide-eyed excited, because I can
recall very little of the chapter explaining
how to write a 5-paragrapher, but that
shining moment covered in shimmer
is clear as summer sunlight, and the
texture of the pages, so slick and so
cool, is ever at my memory's fingertips,
but what I should tell the student
standing in front of me holding a literal
blank sheet of paper and asking me
Where do I even start with this?
eludes me.

Where Do Commas Go?

When I was a small child, I read a
poem in Highlights magazine. I was
an avid reader of Highlights magazine,
for probably too many years past my
young reader cutoff mark, but I didn't
care. I loved it, bright colors, serif fonts,
puzzles I could mull over and ideas I didn't
need to have myself. Avid.

This poem, the one I'm talking about, you
know how they say you remember best
the words that made you angry?

I had never really been made angry by
a written piece before. Being a child
who read children's literature, I had no
acquaintance with inflammatory words,
with comment sections, with those parts
of the Bible where Jesus angers the Pharisees,
who then go forth and spread His Word
but in more of a *Can you believe what
that guy just said?!* way as opposed to
the peaceful dissemination that I think so
many people would like to believe was the
case more often than not, no acquaintance
with that, not yet, but this poem, this one
made me angry.

It was lazy.
It was called *Where Do Butterflies Go
When It Rains?* and I glommed on to it,
eager, because as the child of two science-
trained parents who encouraged me to play
outside, where the nature was, this was a
question I had not considered, and I
thrilled to the idea of learning a new fact
about a world that too often seemed too big
and mysterious to be really knowable.

There was an illustration, a butterfly
hanging upside down beneath a leaf,
while a downpour drenched the world
around it, and yes, I thought, yes, this
will answer nicely.

But no. No. Instead of a tidy poem neatly outlining
the way a butterfly used its gripper feet to
clench itself to a leaf's ridges or veins or
whatever, I got a page of twaddle about
the fragility of life in a universe too often
uncaring.

And I get that the poem is supposed to give
the sensation of where a butterfly goes to
find shelter from disaster, I get that, where,
like, I am the butterfly because children are
vulnerable, or whatever, but I was wanting
more of a, you know, science-based response

to a question I didn't even know I wanted
answered, rather than a flowery illustration
of how it happens, except I just managed
to write that poem myself, wherein I have
used commas where they are supposed
to go in proper usage, and I don't know if that
answers your question.

But that's where commas go.

Period.

Fight the Monster Without Becoming It

It's harder than it looks—I can admit—that—
while swimming through a sea—of clichés—
in student writing—the best they can do. I do—I
know that—I also know—that my training instilled
such a rage against cliché that seeing—so many—
of them hurts—it's a deep physical pain—and part
of my defense against them is writing after work—
writing things which aren't clichés—but are at least—
a little bit—repetitious

OK, Fine, This Is Where Commas Go

You use one to separate dependent clauses, which are phrases that would be sentence fragments if they aren't joined by a comma. They're missing a key piece, such as a subject or verb. They're dependent on each other because they cannot stand alone. You see?

OK, I can see that wasn't a complete explanation. Fine. For example, you'd use a comma to separate an introductory word or phrase. Re-read that last sentence. See, that's how it works. Again, this is how it works. Finally, it works this way.

Let's say you have a list. I don't know how you got the list. It's just a list. OK. You're going to the grocery store, the bank, the dry cleaner's, and someplace else. Yes, you're running errands. Good! You see how that works? Each item gets its own comma after it.

God, it's hard to make this sound instructional and not condescending, and that's on me, not on you. I'm sorry, really.

What about interrupting information? All right. Let's talk about my car. My car, a 1998 Civic, runs just fine, unless the tensioner goes flying off and the belt flops around instead of turning the other end.

Don't worry about the Oxford comma. Serial comma, either. It's the same thing.

Seriously, don't worry about it.

Or, OK, worry about it, but realize—hey, you have children, right? Remember how, before you had children, you thought no one could possibly get so up in arms over whether to feed by bottle or breast, or to stay at home or work once baby is born, or to circumcise or not?

That's the serial comma.

It's a stylistic thing. Style. Hmm. OK. You write papers in MLA for liberal arts classes, and APA for psychology courses, and if you write for a newspaper, you write in AP, or Associated Press. Those are styles. And there's another, Chicago Manual of Style/Turabian, which is essentially the same thing. It has footnotes. People love that. Well, some people. So in some styles, you use the serial comma, and in others, it is forbidden, except in cases where understanding would be clouded without it. Frankly, I don't think that really helps, because *I had my godparents, Barack Obama and Oprah* clearly needs that serial comma, where *I bought bananas, peanuts and butter* might or might not trip a reader up.

But it's not just a style concern. To some people, it's a rallying cry, a beacon, a hill to die on. You? Probably you just need to worry about whether the people reading your paper can figure out what you're talking about.

I Finally Understand

God helps those who help themselves is
on a loop in my head as I stare at a student's
forehead, trying to avoid eye contact while
still appearing to pay attention, because if
I make eye contact, I will interrupt the barrage
of excuses and questions. I am wearied by the
energy this student is pouring into the problem,
whatever it is, because this energy isn't a
solution, it's only tangling it worse, but I am
certainly not about to tell anyone that. No
sir. I cannot help them help themselves.

Fault Line

But Marybeth, if I don't ace this quiz,
I'll fail the class, and that will be your
fault!

First of all, I point out in my
best educator voice, *I am here to help
you, but I cannot build a bridge where no
footings have been poured, and no
supplies have been shipped in, and no
workers have been hired, much less
advertised for, and the architect's
plans lie neglected in a dusty office
somewhere whose single light is zapping
on and off, intermittently, OK?*

I get a blank stare in response. Of course.

Let's try this again, I say, managing
not to rub the bridge of my nose.

Did you read the chapter? No. *Did
you ace the quiz before this one?* No.
Did you take the quiz before this one?
No. *Did you read any of the chapters
before this one?* No. *Did you turn in
your assignments?* No. *Do you have
your textbook?* No. *What week of*

the semester are we in? Twelve. *Have you asked me any questions at all this semester?*
I could ask questions?

So you are trying to blame me for your lack of preparation.
Blank stare.

Are you familiar with cause-effect relationships?

Is that where...something happens... because of something else?

Why yes.

Okayyy...

If you prepare for a quiz, you are more likely to do well on it. Okayyy... How do you prepare for a quiz? Blank stare.

And that's when I remember that line about leading a horse to water and pushing its head into the water and holding it there until it either drinks or drowns, or I might not be remembering that right.

My fault, my ass

Roundabout

This isn't how it used to be. At least, I don't
think it is. It's hard to remember. Been a few
years. I used to drive these roads in my
teenage frenzy, my version of *Breakfast
at Tiffany's*, only instead of Audrey in an
LBD with beignets and mean reds, it was
a gawky blonde teenager in a Skankin' Pickle
t-shirt and a Geo Metro.

So, kind of the same, in a roundabout way.

Speaking of roundabout ways, and sameness
being not really at all the case, I was going
somewhere with this.

This isn't how it used to be. I've been through
Fredericktown since I was a teenager, sure.
It's been twenty years and while
I don't always have business this way, I am
usually up for a meandering journey to nowhere
really. Not that Fredericktown is nowhere really.
Dammit. Let me start again.

This isn't how it used to be. I was driving this
way for the fourteenth time this semester, and
on a happenstance glance to my right, I saw
the remains of a highway in a farmer's field.

Fascinating. It was pinkish asphalt, overgrown
with weeds and probably soybeans (hard to tell
at fifty miles per hour), and it hit me—the
pinkish rock quarried from deposits near here,
up by Elephant Rock State Park and
Johnson's Shut-Ins, which I thought
were the most romantic and odd names
until I actually went there.
Then it made all kinds of sense.

But that pinkish asphalt reminded me that the terrain
isn't the same as it was when I first drove through here,
on my way to the summer camp where I'd meet the guy
who later hired me to work this very job.

Is the terrain different, or am I?

It sounds like an obvious question, the sort of answer
that thrums in the air behind it. *Of course I am different*,
I want to be able to say, and have it be the truth, but here,
in my green Civic rocket-powered by my ambition and
gas at a little over a dollar a gallon, nothing seems like
obvious truth.

This is different, the way the roads lay now. Intersections
and a few different routes that'll take you exactly where
your little heart guides you, I had noticed that much.
OO takes you from Junction City up through Mine La
Motte, which name I am delighted by but have never
bothered to look up until just now.

Turns out, like almost every small town
around here, it's named after a mine named after a guy
whose name isn't quite the same as the town.

That's the way to Farmington, OO, your shoulderless
alternative to four-lane 67, with its higher speed limit
and safety features like guardrails and open areas near
the road so you can see things like flocks of turkeys
before running them over, for instance. It's about the
same distance, but takes a little longer.

I usually prefer 67, since I drive like a grandmother
and I feel badly for other drivers stuck behind me,
but 67 takes me through the roundabout, and I'm
less inclined to love the roundabout. These started
to pop up all over southeastern Missouri within the
last fifteen years or so. I'm guessing someone at
MODOT just *really loves* how they look in traffic
reduction simulators, if those are actually a thing.
I can't say I have a lot of experience in government
offices.

But I will say this for roundabouts, they're
definitely good for increasing the terror quotient of any
drive through town, so there's that.

But I think something happened. This isn't how it was.
I think they changed 72 when they put this roundabout
in. I think 72 used to be the pinkish asphalt now littering
that farmer's field. I think 72 used to meander through
Fredericktown's business district. I think I remember

having to turn left at Junction City to get north of
Fredericktown by going through Fredericktown.
67 and 72 crossed, but I think there were
turns to make to different places, like a subdivision back
behind Walmart and maybe there were other places too,
but I wasn't a native, just an occasional visitor, not even
a proper commuter, if there is such a thing.

Now, though, this isn't how it was. No, no,
now there's a two-lane road that connects OO and the
roundabout, and the signs say that two-lane road with a
50 mph speed limit is actually 72.

I tried, one afternoon, to take a detour through
Fredericktown. I wanted to see the Square again, with its
on-road parking, its hilarious speed limit (something like
20, I think). I also wondered how many businesses I
remembered were still there.

Turns out mostly none.

But the Junction City area was a little different than I
remembered. More For Sale signs, more adverts for
home businesses. I guess an hour commute to the
nearest decent-sized city (Cape Girardeau, for you
at home keeping score) is a little much in these modern
times of high-speed internet and higher gas prices.

Junction City

I have never felt more as though I am
a dolphin in a redneck tuna net
as when I drive through this place
and see the signs casting about
for customers, none of whom
are me. It kills me.
I do not want to drive down a
somehow-dark-in-broad-daylight alley
at the beckoning of a hand-painted sign
for *Live Bait*.
I can't vote for any of these local
politicians. I would, of course,
vote for Wayne Spain, as his name
rhymes, though it isn't spelled
the way I would've spelled it.
Also,
I don't need an auction company,
or a backyard shed,
or even a stop at Hardee's
only 39 miles from home.

To the Man in the Blue Neon with Wide White Stripes

I know, I'm sorry, I'm not up on my paint-job lingo. I don't know what the term is for those stripes. I'm sure there is one. Not that it matters, exactly, since I have no interest in actually speaking to you. You're scowling every time I see you, frowning, grizzled face shadowed by your car's visor, squinting into the sun, sans sunglasses. I don't really understand, but perhaps I'm not meant to. I see you every day, you know, here, on this stretch of MO-72 West. I've been on the road since 4:00, and here it is, 4:48, and I see you, your fish lure of a car whose license plate I've memorized, not that it matters, exactly. I'm tired. I'm hypnotized by an indifferent, twisted highway, lonesome as I am right now. Cell coverage is spotty out this way so I've learned to entertain myself on the drive. I listen to NPR's halfway-crabby coverage of issues that are supposed to be relevant to me. I feel the judgment of my inattention to the world out there, in Ari Shapiro's smug yet shmexy voice. I'm sad because he calls all the female correspondents by the diminutive forms of their names, yet I've never heard him refer to Robert Siegel as Bob. But Lourdes Garcia Navarro is totally LuLu. Gross. And there you are. There you are, driving home, again, I guess, unless you're on your way to a five o'clock shift in Fredericktown. I don't even know if Fredericktown has anyplace with a five o'clock shift, and anyway, this particular stretch is a few more than twelve minutes away from there, unless of course you're

driving over the speed limit, which, hey, I mean,
everyone does on this road, am I right? I never see a state
 trooper but that might have more to do with how this
 damn road has a foot of shoulder, which makes
me giggle because foot and shoulder are both body parts
 too, and I think about how everyone driving here has
 their own body they inhabit, a spirit extending
into flesh, into vehicle, all on their way to something or
from someone, and I round the uphill corner just a few
 miles on, drive past the factory where

> I bet you work,
> and you're off
> shift at 4:30.

Sliding Doors

I've seen it more often than I've seen actual doors, sliding, probably. Almost like it's more my DNA than a British film from 1998.

I first watched it that summer I was twenty, before my life became some slant parody of the storylines. I identified with Gwyneth Paltrow's Helen, not as a successful up and comer, working in a PR firm, London, no, not as that so much, but the blonde in twin storylines, eerily similar to what would come to pass for me maybe twelve years later. Hundreds, many hundreds of times, I watched the movie, two hours at a time over years, a decade, more years still, and every time the nasal British *Hay-uve fun, ah-livin' in the cit-tay* opening theme played over stock footage of the Thames and a typical London morning, I felt the weird parallel to my own existence, an ambitious blonde who doesn't have the moxie to realize her own potential, so takes a string of terrible jobs to keep money coming in, while her live-in doofus works on an endless novel, except I'm the one writing a perpetual novel, but it's an actual novel, not a sad cover for some naked midday tryst-o-thon. And while you, my *James,* are not a Scotsman who owns a company, complete with doors sliding in and out of place, so as to further the metaphor, you see, you do quote Monty Python kind of a lot, for real.

And I showed that movie to you, almost shamefaced, like I had a hard-held secret and I wasn't sure you'd care. I should have known better. I sat on the couch, holding a pillow on my lap, not moving, staring hard at the movie spooling out on your big screen, and every time you looked at me, you'd ask, *Did ... did they write this ... about you?* And I just kept saying, *I knew it was my life, and yet I did nothing,* but each time I'd say that, you'd just shake your head and point out to me that if I had done anything, I might not have met you, and that's why everything had to happen the way it did.

No Line

There's been some construction on Highway 72.
They're widening the lanes, adding a tiny shoulder,
resurfacing pavement gone gray and cracked. Needed
improvements, MoDOT said, probably. They added
those little plastic reflective jobs to indicate center
stripes, and the outer edges of each lane are ribbed
to remind drivers where to drive. They've even painted
stripes, which is a little silly to my thinking, because
this two-lane highway winds and twists over hills
and through forests.

I wouldn't consider passing anyone ever, not even
a farmer moving equipment, because let's be real
here, I knew someone who hit another driver head-on
out here and almost died, broke her wrist and spiked
her insurance premiums, adding financial insult to
serious physical harm, so that feels like a risk
I don't want to take.

But they all feel that way to me, these days. I
used to be an aggressive driver, taking offense
at every turn, but that ended. Couple of tickets,
wrecks, I decided not to live my life that way.
I retreated.

You would think I would want the lines, want to
know where the borders are, but I'm fine without them.

Of course, MoDOT thinks I still need the signs.

NO CENTER LINE, they say, comfortingly,
orangely, every ten miles.

NO CENTER LINE, they say, exactly where the
center line already is. I think about this, wonderingly,
remembering what life was like in those first few
months after the divorce.

NO CENTER LINE, they say, and I remember catching
myself as if falling, fumbling to figure out where to
apologize, crying not from sadness but because
the new emotions were just too big to hold in.

NO CENTER LINE, and there was promise of a new
existence, an existence free from worrying I was wrong
about everything (literally everything, you don't even
know—my hair wasn't washed often enough, my tone of
voice was off-putting, I was being annoying, I was not
thinking of others, I was thinking too much of others, I
wasn't speaking up enough, I was talking too much,
I was showing off, I was being too modest, and on and
on and ON AND ON AND ON), and I did
not know what to do with myself, because

NO CENTER LINE, and I KNOW there's a center line
but every sign tells me there isn't one, and if that isn't
the most perfect metaphor for life after divorce, then
maybe, maybe there isn't a better one.

Don't Half Ass Your Cheatery

Or if you're going to cheat, at least don't
insult my intelligence. Of course, I realize
your cheating isn't about me. I don't factor
into your equation at all, as I'm not much
more than a nebulous concept to you. You
could be standing in the living room after
a night of drinking and whatever else, or
in the writing lab, explaining why the font
changed in the middle of your paper that
was clearly one sentence of your writing
and eleven sentences from a fan page
about exactly what your paper was about,
and I can know that by *using Google*, because
I know how to copy and paste, too. You have
the same facial expression, the same hangdog
posture, the same pretended defeat by monogamy
or making sentences, or maybe I'm just cynical,
or, you know, good at sticking with what I've said
I will do.

But if you're going to cheat, you should at least
put some effort into it.

You've heard of the trickster god? Loki? Bugs
Bunny? Descartes' evil genius, the being who
could easily be corrupting the information you're
getting from your senses? OK, Bugs Bunny, at least.

Be a low-key Loki. Impress me with your cheating.
The artistry you use should rival the caper at
the beginning of every movie that makes you
root for the villains. Build a cathedral to your
cheating. *Commit.*

Don't make your cheating an insult to the
process. Try to trick me, but not by copy-paste
Wikipedia. No. Trick me by skipping around
the edges of the assignment guidelines, fulfilling
the requirements, but, like, *technically.*

Just remember: the trickster god generally wins,
and if he doesn't win, he's at least entertaining
to watch.
As he dies.
With an F.
Descartes' evil genius is not you, son.

Stomping Grounds
for Daniel Crocker

That's my old stomping grounds, Dan Crocker says when I tell him I'm teaching in Park Hills, which borders Crocker's hometown. I'm reminded of the first time I met Dan Crocker, the first real poet I'd ever met, who at the time had three books of poetry published. I was almost 19, dipping my toe in the creative-writing scene at Southeast Missouri State University, at the time an insular group more interested in the Beat lifestyle than crafting poetry people would actually want to read, or at least that's how I remember it.

But when Crocker was introduced and gave a sheepish *Yes, three books, that sounds right*, I sat up a little straighter. This guy studying for a master's degree in the very halls where I was first touching the talent I'd later nudge into something publishable, wearing a flannel shirt and jeans and close-cut dark hair and wire-rim glasses, he read poems in plain language that nevertheless elevated his subjects to more than pedestrian, and I was hooked.

I lost track of Crocker through the years, along with a lot of other compass points that were distant but nonetheless fixtures, but occasionally I'd hear he had another book out, or was studying for his doctorate in another state, or was involved in some prestigious project or other. I cheered him on, in silence.

The sea change in my life that dropped me, wrecked
and nervous, on the shores of the master's program,
also landed me at a table in a bar where I was
introduced around to faculty I'd be studying with.
I was already a little too gone when I met Crocker,
finally, managing not to tell him any of this, not the
admiration I had for his work from the first; not the
delight I found in seeing a poet who felt comfortable,
even confident, in producing work that felt raw and
honest and real in a way the glib nonsense from
the Beat admirers never touched; instead I mumbled
into my bottle of Stag that I'd heard him read one
time, and had liked it, and much to my surprise he
laughed and thanked me, then said he'd look forward
to working with me.

That guy!

Every Fry a Bag Fry

There's a certain romance to
bag fries—the lone strips of
fried potato, jostling together
but apart, drifting between
napkin and cheeseburger,
growing cold and mealy by
the moment, dotting the brown
paper with smears of darker
brown, evading my fingertips
as I dig through the bag doing
73 in a 70

The Moon Rocks Over

The hillside's dewy tonight, and cold
while the moon rocks over us all. I haven't
seen the stars so sharp as they are tonight
in years. It's as though they're seeing me
as much as I'm seeing them, with new clarity,
which is a touch unsettling, to speak truth on
the subject.

But the moon rocks over us all
and softens imperfections daylight seems
to revel in revealing. I could watch it do its
thing for hours on end, never once looking away,
which is the biggest advantage the moon has
over the sun, in my estimation, though the night
has appeals beyond the soft moon and diamond-
bright stars, they shine while the moon rocks
over us all. The cattle low and grasses rustle while
I drive by, watching, thinking. It's how I do, long hours
feel slower, long thoughts go deeper, and I feel myself
pulling into the hillside almost as much as it's pulling

Marybeth Niederkorn is an award-winning journalist, essayist, and author. Educated at Southeast Missouri State University, she holds a bachelor's degree in philosophy and a master's in professional writing, but tries not to be a jerk about it. She lives in Missouri with her awesome husband, Dave, and their two obstreperous cats. This is her first book.

This project was made possible, in part, by generous support from the Osage Arts Community.

Osage Arts Community provides temporary time, space and support for the creation of new artistic works in a retreat format, serving creative people of all kinds — visual artists, composers, poets, fiction and nonfiction writers. Located on a 152-acre farm in an isolated rural mountainside setting in Central Missouri and bordered by ¾ of a mile of the Gasconade River, OAC provides residencies to those working alone, as well as welcoming collaborative teams, offering living space and workspace in a country environment to emerging and mid-career artists. For more information, visit us at www.osageac.org

www.ingramcontent.com/pod-product-compliance
Lightning Source LLC
Chambersburg PA
CBHW020128130526
44591CB00032B/573